The Battle of Gettysburg

by Michael Burgan

Content Adviser: Professor Sherry L. Field,
Department of Social Science Education, College of Education,
The University of Georgia

Reading Adviser: Dr. Linda D. Labbo,
Department of Reading Education, College of Education,
The University of Georgia

COMPASS POINT BOOKS

Minneapolis, Minnesota

Photographs ©: Stock Montage, cover, 7, 14, 26, 35; Medford Historical Society Collection/ Corbis, 4; North Wind Picture Archives, 5, 6, 10, 20, 28, 36; Visuals Unlimited, 8; Corbis, 9, 13, 38; Archive Photos, 11, 21, 23, 30, 34; Library of Congress, 12 (left and right), 15, 16, 19, 25, 27, 29, 32, 33, 39; Steve Strickland/ Visuals Unlimited; Timothy H. O'Sullivan/George Eastman House/Archive Photos, 22; David Muench/Corbis, 24; XNR Production, Inc., 31; Imperial War Museum/Archive Photos, 37; Hulton Getty/Archive Photos, 40; William B. Folsom, 41.

Editors: E. Russell Primm and Emily J. Dolbear
Photo Researcher: Svetlana Zhurkina
Photo Selector: Linda S. Koutris
Designer: Bradfordesign, Inc.

Library of Congress Cataloging-in-Publication Data

Burgan, Michael.
    The Battle of Gettysburg / by Michael Burgan.
        p. cm. — (We the people)
    Includes bibliographical references and index.
    ISBN 0-7565-0098-2 (lib. bdg.)
        1. Gettysburg (Pa.), Battle of, 1863—Juvenile literature. [1. Gettysburg (Pa.), Battle of, 1863.
2. United States—History—Civil War, 1861–1865—Campaigns.] I. Title. II. We the people
(Compass Point Books)
    E475.53 .B96 2001
    973.7'349—dc21

00-011015

TABLE OF CONTENTS

SHOES FOR THE TROOPS

Just before noon on June 30, 1863, General John Buford led his Union troops into the town of Gettysburg, Pennsylvania. Buford's **cavalry** was the first wave of the advancing Northern army. When he arrived, Buford learned that the Southern troops had just left town.

General John Buford of the Union army

From outside Gettysburg, General James Pettigrew, commander of the departed Confederate, or Southern, troops, reported to his superiors. He had gone to Gettysburg to get

4

A member of the Union cavalry

much-needed shoes for his soldiers. He left—
without the shoes—when he saw the Northern
horsemen approaching. Pettigrew reported that
the Union forces had entered Gettysburg. General
Henry Heth did not believe the report, however.
He said, "I will take my division and go down
there and get the shoes myself." He planned to
leave the next day.

Preparing for battle

That night, the people of Gettysburg saw fires burning all around their town. The flickering yellow lights marked the campgrounds of the Northern and Southern forces. General Buford knew that a battle was coming. "The enemy will attack us in the morning," he told another officer, "and we will have to fight like devils." The opposing armies were about to wage the single greatest battle of the Civil War—the Battle of Gettysburg.

6

BEFORE THE BATTLE

The Civil War had started in 1861, more than two years earlier. Its roots, tied to the problems of slavery, went even farther back in history. For decades, many Northerners had opposed slavery. Some wanted to stop its spread to new states. Others hoped to end it completely. In the South, slave owners argued that they needed the slaves to work on their **plantations**. Many Southerners also

Southern plantations relied on slave labor.

7

President Abraham Lincoln

disliked the idea that the federal government could tell the states what to do.

In 1860, Abraham Lincoln was elected the sixteenth president of the United States. Lincoln opposed the spread of slavery. Many Southern slave owners feared that Lincoln and other Northerners would now try to end slavery.

Soon after Lincoln's election, eleven slave states seceded, or broke away, from the Union to form their own country. These Southern states called themselves the Confederate States of America. Lincoln refused to accept the separation of the Southern states, however. "No state," he

8

said, "upon its own mere notion, can lawfully get out of the Union."

The political conflict between the Northern and Southern states soon turned into a war. On April 12, 1861, Confederate troops attacked and took control of Fort Sumter in South Carolina. Lincoln called for 75,000 volunteers to join the Union army. These soldiers would fight against the rebel army of the Confederacy.

Fort Sumter, South Carolina

Confederate troops prepare to defend the South.

Northern and Southern troops first met on the battlefield in Virginia. Gradually, the Civil War spread across the southern half of the country.

The Confederacy's strategy was to defend its own territory. At times, however, Confederate troops attacked Union troops. The Union's goal was to take control of important Southern cities and destroy the Confederate army. By the middle of 1863, the North was making gains in the West, along the Mississippi River. On battlefields in the East, both armies won victories.

The Southern army in the East was called the Army of Northern Virginia. Its commander, General Robert E. Lee, wanted to win a major victory on Northern soil. Lee thought that a victory in the North would break his enemy's spirit.

General Robert E. Lee of the Confederate army

He also thought that an attack in the North might force the Union to move its troops there—and out of the Mississippi River region—to defend the land. Lee also wanted to take food and supplies from the territory he captured. In early June 1863, Lee began to move his troops from Virginia toward Pennsylvania.

The Union army that was fighting in Virginia was called the Army of the Potomac.

11

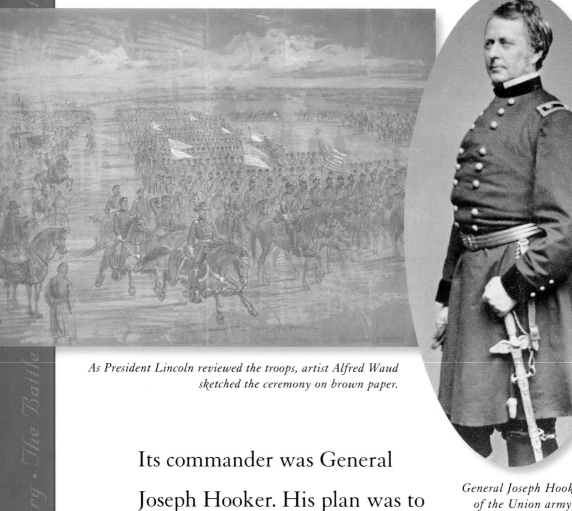

As President Lincoln reviewed the troops, artist Alfred Waud sketched the ceremony on brown paper.

General Joseph Hooker of the Union army

Its commander was General Joseph Hooker. His plan was to keep his troops between Lee's advancing forces and the city of Washington, D.C. But Hooker did not take any major steps to fight Lee's army as it marched north.

12

THE ROAD TO GETTYSBURG

General Lee's Confederate army was divided into three large units called corps. He also had a cavalry unit, which was led by General J. E. B. Stuart. A daring, dashing figure on horseback, Stuart commanded almost 10,000 well-trained soldiers. These cavalry troops often acted as scouts,

General J. E. B. Stuart of the Confederate army

reporting on the position of Union forces.

By mid-June, all three of General Lee's corps were on the move. Along the way, Southern troops sometimes fought with Northern troops. General Richard Ewell and his Confederate corps took

13

*General Richard Ewell
of the Confederate army*

more than 3,000 Union prisoners in a battle at Winchester, Virginia. This victory gave the Confederates a clear path across the Potomac River into the North.

On June 21, Ewell's corps entered Chambersburg, Pennsylvania—just west of Gettysburg. A few days later, Lee's other two corps reached Pennsylvania. They took food and horses from the farms scattered around the countryside. One Confederate soldier wrote to his wife, "We are paying back these people for some of the damage they have done us, though we are not doing them half as bad as they done us." The soldier added, "We will have to fight here, and when it

14

comes it will be the biggest on record."

The Confederate troops in Pennsylvania were somewhat scattered, but Lee was not worried. He felt safe, believing that General Hooker's Union army still had not crossed the Potomac River. Lee did not realize it, but his scouts were too far away to report quickly—which meant that the general did not know the truth.

Union cavalrymen approach Gettysburg.

15

Confederate forces under the command of General Stuart

A few days earlier, the cavalry's general, Stuart, had asked Lee's permission to ride east, around the Northern army. Lee agreed. Stuart, however, did not realize how much area the Union forces had covered. The scouts had to ride a long distance from Lee's main force. Stuart and his soldiers finally learned that Hooker's troops had crossed the Potomac River. By then, they were too far away for this news to reach Lee quickly. For days, Lee didn't know where his enemy was.

On June 28, Union troops gathered near Frederick, Maryland—about 30 miles (48 kilometers) from the Pennsylvania border. That day, a Confederate spy finally told Lee the position of the Union troops. The spy also informed Lee that General Hooker was no longer the commander of the Union's Army of the Potomac.

Earlier that day, President Lincoln had replaced Hooker with George Meade. Lincoln felt that Hooker did not have the skills needed to win a major battle against General Lee. Hooker had done badly in a previous battle. Lincoln now hoped that General Meade could stop the Confederate advance.

Lee was not happy about the change in Union leadership. He had counted on Hooker to make mistakes on the battlefield, as he had done before.

General George Meade of the Union army

The Confederate commander told his staff, "General Meade will make no blunder in my front, and if I make one, he will make haste to take advantage of it."

Lee figured the two armies would meet somewhere near Gettysburg. He ordered his troops to gather in that region. Meade also saw this area as a likely battle spot, but most of his troops were still in Maryland. He ordered General Buford and his cavalry into Gettysburg to watch for the Confederate movement. The two armies prepared for another battle.

THE FIRST DAY

Early in the morning of July 1, 1863, General Heth led Confederate troops into Gettysburg. When shots rang out, Heth realized that the Union forces had indeed

Both the Union and Confederate armies fought with cannons during the Battle of Gettysburg.

reached town—just as General Pettigrew had reported the day before. General Heth gathered his troops on Herr Ridge. Soon, Union **artillery** guns rang out. Cannon balls and exploding shells hit the Southern troops. Buford's soldiers jumped off their horses and began firing their fast-loading rifles— but they were outnumbered. The general quickly called for help.

Union infantry

Soon, more troops from both sides poured into Gettysburg and the surrounding countryside. Infantry—foot soldiers—attacked while moving into better positions. Artillery guns boomed, cutting down advancing troops.

Augustus Buell belonged to a Union artillery unit. He described the sights and sounds of battle: "Up and down the line men reeling and falling; splinters flying from wheels and axles where bullets hit; in rear, horses tearing and plunging, mad with wounds or terror; drivers yelling, shells bursting, shot shrieking overhead, howling about our ears or throwing up great clouds of dust where they struck."

Cemetery Hill

By afternoon, General Lee had reached Herr Ridge and was watching the battle. He had not wanted to fight there because he still was not sure where the rest of Meade's troops were. However, the battle had begun and the Southern troops were fighting well. The Union troops moved back, seeking high ground. They gathered on Cemetery Hill and, farther east, on Culp's Hill. Lee had ordered General Ewell to take Cemetery Hill if he

21

Dead soldiers lie on the battlefield at Gettysburg.

could—but Ewell had hesitated, and the Union soldiers took it first.

The first day at Gettysburg was devastating for the Union army. It had almost 10,000 casualties—soldiers wounded, killed, missing, or captured. Now, after taking Cemetery Hill and Culp's Hill, the Union forces were in a stronger defensive position. Still, Lee was ready for another day's battle. He pointed to the hills where the Northern troops had dug in. "The enemy is there," Lee said, "and I am going to attack him there."

THE SECOND DAY

During the night, General Meade arrived at Gettysburg from Taneytown, Maryland. The next morning, he was tired but determined. Another general asked the Union leader how many of his troops would be ready to fight. Meade replied,

General Meade of the Union army prepares for battle.

The headquarters of General Meade

"I expect to have about 95,000—enough, I guess, for this business. . . . We may fight it out here just as well as anywhere else."

More Union troops arrived, and Meade was waiting for still others. Many of the Union soldiers lined up on Cemetery Ridge, just in front of Cemetery Hill. Others spread out behind them, southeast of Culp's Hill.

A Union corps led by General Daniel Sickles was supposed to take a hill just south of Cemetery Ridge. The hill was called Little Round Top. South of that hill was a larger hill called Round Top. Sickles examined the area but decided on another position. He chose a

General Daniel Sickles
of the Union army

spot in front of Little Round Top, where a peach orchard stood. Sickles waited for Meade to reply to his request to change position. When no answer came, Sickles acted on his own. He positioned the Union troops in the peach orchard, leaving the two Round Tops undefended.

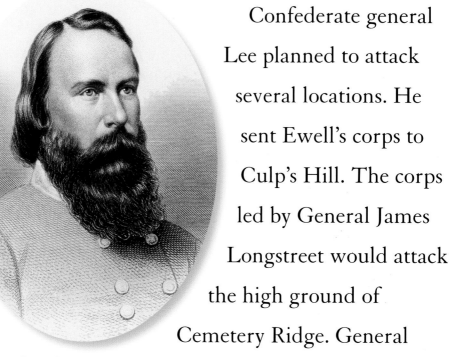

General James Longstreet of the Confederate army

Confederate general Lee planned to attack several locations. He sent Ewell's corps to Culp's Hill. The corps led by General James Longstreet would attack the high ground of Cemetery Ridge. General A. P. Hill and his corps would head for the center of the Union position.

General John Hood led some Confederate troops toward the peach orchard and a nearby wheat field. But General Sickles had already moved his Union troops there, so Hood sought a new location. He sent his troops to the undefended hills—Round Top and Little Round Top.

The battle at a site called Peach Orchard

A few Union sharpshooters fired down on the approaching soldiers from Round Top, but the Confederates stormed up the hill. When General Hood was wounded in the fighting, Colonel William Oates continued to lead the Southern troops up Round Top. Oates also wanted to move cannons up the hill. From the top of the hill, the

27

A sharpshooter takes aim.

guns would be in a good position to fire down on the Union troops. Before he could act, however, Oates received an order to leave Round Top and head for Little Round Top.

By this time, Union officers realized that Little Round Top was undefended. Northern troops scrambled up the hill before the Confederates could reach it. Colonel Joshua Chamberlain led the Union defense of the hill. Some of his soldiers were volunteers from Maine. They were trained as fishers and lumberjacks, not as fighters—but the Union forces held off the rebels. They finally used their bayonets to drive off the attacking soldiers. The victory at Little Round Top was one of the most important Union victories of the day.

Other battles raged. General Sickles's Union troops and Longstreet's Confederates fought for control of the wheat field. Sickles's troops were lined up in a **salient,** a line of defense that forms an angle. This position left them open to attack from two sides. Sickles himself was wounded and later had to have his leg

As the Civil War continued, volunteer troops were needed.

29

Devil's Den

removed. Fierce fighting also took place in the rocks at Devil's Den—a large patch of boulders in front of Little Round Top.

When that day was over, the North held its key positions on the high ground. Still, Lee was ready to attack again. The Union had many casualties, and the Southern troops had driven back the Union troops in some areas. Lee thought he could win with one last major attack. Meanwhile, on the battlefield, the cries of the wounded cut through the quiet of the night.

The Battle of Gettysburg

Legend:

- ✹ Battle site
- **CONFEDERATE FORCES**
  - ← Lee
  - ◄– Stuart
  - ◄··· Lee's retreat
- **UNION FORCES**
  - ← Hooker
  - ◄– Meade

Condoguinet Creek · Susquehanna

P e n n s y l v a n i a

Chambersburg · Gettysburg · Taneytown

West Virginia · Williamsport · Hagerstown · Monocacy · Westminster

Antietam Cr. · Shepherdstown · Frederick · M a r y l a n d

Shenandoah · Winchester · Potomac

V i r g i n i a

N

0 25 50 miles
0 25 50 kilometers

THE THIRD DAY

Lee's plan was to send about 12,500 Southern troops into the center of the Union line. General Long-street opposed the plan. He thought the Confe-derate troops were doomed to fail. Lee refused to change his mind, however. Longstreet later wrote, "Never was I so depressed as upon that day."

Lee planned to begin his attack with a huge

During the battle, artist Alfred Waud sketched the action on brown paper.

The Union army used cannons to fight the Confederate troops.

artillery **barrage**. He had about 170 pieces of artillery ready for battle—but before the South could launch its attack, the North struck first. Union cannons fired down on General Ewell's troops near Culp's Hill. The rebels fought back, and the battle raged on for three hours. Out-numbered, the Confederate troops finally retreated.

At 1 P.M., Lee's main force was ready to attack. The South's cannons suddenly opened fire, and the North's guns responded. This artillery battle was the largest of the Civil War. A New York journalist on the scene wrote: "The storm broke upon us so suddenly that soldiers and officers . . . died, some with cigars between their teeth, some with pieces of food in their fingers." Smoke soon covered the battlefield. Explosions erupted as shells blew up supplies of **ammunition**.

When the guns stopped firing, the Confederate infantry moved in. Leading one wave of these soldiers was General George Pickett. The entire infantry assault was later known as Pickett's

The fighting at Gettysburg was fierce.

Pickett's Charge

Charge. The rebels' target was a stand of trees near the center of Cemetery Ridge. In front of the trees was a stone fence. The fence ran south, turned west for more than 200 feet (61 meters), then headed south again. Behind that stone fence, Northern troops waited.

The Confederate troops tried to overwhelm their enemy but were cut down by streams of bullets and artillery. When Union troops fell, others quickly rushed in to replace them. Confederate general Lewis Armistead roared across the stone

*General Lewis Armistead
of the Confederate army*

fence, with his sword drawn, "Come on, boys," he shouted. "Give them the cold steel. Who will follow me?"—But he was shot before he could attack. Some Confederate soldiers did reach the stone fence, however. The fighting at the corner of the fence was so fierce that the spot was later called the Bloody Angle.

Northern forces continued to cut down the advancing rebels. A Northern reporter described the scene: "The ground is thick with dead, and the wounded are like the withered leaves of autumn. Thousands of rebels throw down their arms and give themselves up as prisoners." In the end, the Confederate troops were not able to break through the Union defenses. Lee's plan had failed.

AFTER THE BATTLE

July 4, 1863, was not a happy Independence Day for either side. The battle was over, and the two armies counted their losses. The North had suffered more than 23,000 casualties, about 25 percent of its total force. The South had lost as many as 28,000 men—about 40 percent of its troops.

More than 50,000 men died at Gettysburg.

37

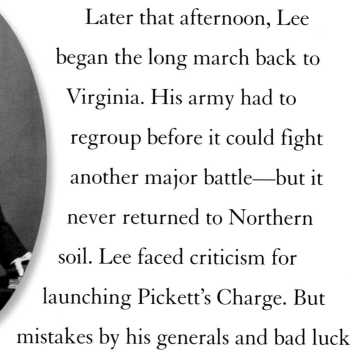

Jefferson Davis

Later that afternoon, Lee began the long march back to Virginia. His army had to regroup before it could fight another major battle—but it never returned to Northern soil. Lee faced criticism for launching Pickett's Charge. But mistakes by his generals and bad luck had a large part in the defeat. Still, after the loss, Lee said, "It was my fault this time." He offered to quit his post as commander of the rebel forces. The Confederate president, Jefferson Davis, refused his offer.

When Lee withdrew from Gettysburg, Meade did not chase him down. President Lincoln was furious when he heard this report. He had wanted

38

Meade to crush Lee's army when he had the chance. Later, Meade also offered to quit. Despite his anger, Lincoln did not accept Meade's offer—but the president continued to look for a general who would be willing to destroy Lee's forces.

In and around Gettysburg, the hills and fields were littered with the dead. Thousands of dead soldiers were barely covered with earth. A local banker, David Wills, noted how poorly the bodies

Thousands of horses and mules were also killed during combat.

39

President Lincoln gave the Gettysburg Address in 1863.

were buried. He led the efforts to give dead
soldiers from both sides decent burials. About
5,000 horses and mules also died during the
fighting. Their bodies were burned.

Wills raised money to buy land, and in
October, the dead were reburied in a new military
cemetery. The next month, Wills scheduled a
ceremony to honor those killed at Gettysburg.
President Lincoln agreed to say a few words
during the ceremony. On November 19, Lincoln

gave one of the most famous speeches in American history—the Gettysburg Address—to a gathering of about 15,000 people.

In his speech, President Lincoln said that the soldiers had made the cemetery ground a **sacred** place by sacrificing their lives. He asked the audience to carry on the mission of the dead, to keep their country united and free, so that the "government of the people, by the people, and for the people shall not **perish** from the earth." For many, Lincoln's words helped to ease the memory of the horror and bloodshed that took place at Gettysburg.

A memorial to both Union and Confederate soldiers who died in battle

41

GLOSSARY

ammunition—bullets and shells for guns

artillery—large guns mounted on wheels, such as cannons

barrage—heavy gunfire

cavalry—soldiers who ride horses into battle

perish—die

plantations—large farms that grow one main crop such as cotton

sacred—holy or deserving great respect

salient—a line of defense that projects farthest toward the enemy

DID YOU KNOW?

- Confederate soldiers never advanced farther north than Pennsylvania.

- General Daniel Sickles of the Union army saved the bones from his amputated leg and sent them to the Army Medical Museum in Washington, D.C. After the war, he often went to see the bones.

- It cost $1.59 per body to rebury the dead at the Gettysburg cemetery.

- Abraham Lincoln's famous Gettysburg Address is only 272 words long. It took the president about three minutes to deliver it.

IMPORTANT DATES

Timeline

1860	Abraham Lincoln is elected the sixteenth U.S. president on November 6; South Carolina becomes the first Southern state to secede from the Union on December 20.
1861	The Civil War begins at Fort Sumter, South Carolina, on April 12; the first major battle of the war takes place in Virginia on July 21.
1863	In May, General Robert E. Lee of the Confederate army wins a major battle at Chancellorsville, Virginia; in June, General Lee moves his forces northward into Pennsylvania; the Battle of Gettysburg is fought from July 1 to July 3; President Lincoln delivers the Gettysburg Address on November 19.
1865	The South surrenders; the Civil War ends.

IMPORTANT PEOPLE

LEWIS ARMISTEAD
(1817–1863), *Confederate general who was killed at Gettysburg*

JOSHUA CHAMBERLAIN
(1828–1914), *victorious Union colonel at Little Round Top*

JOSEPH HOOKER
(1814–1879), *Union army general*

ROBERT E. LEE
(1807–1870), *Confederate army general*

GEORGE MEADE
(1815–1872), *Union army general in charge at Gettysburg*

GEORGE PICKETT
(1825–1875), *Confederate army general*

DANIEL SICKLES
(1825–1914), *Union army general wounded during the Battle of Gettysburg*

J. E. B. STUART
(1833–1864), *Confederate army general who led Lee's cavalry unit*

WANT TO KNOW MORE?

At the Library

Cannon, Marian G. *Robert E. Lee: Defender of the South.* New York: Franklin
  Watts, 1993.

Corrick, James A. *The Battle of Gettysburg.* San Diego: Lucent Books, 1996.

Hughes, Christopher A. *Gettysburg.* New York: Twenty-First Century
  Books, 1998.

Kallen, Stuart A. *The Gettysburg Address.* Edina, Minn.: Abdo and
  Daughters, 1994.

On the Web

The Gettysburg Address

http://www.lcweb.loc.gov/exhibits/gadd/

For President Abraham Lincoln's first and final drafts of his speech

Civil War Times—Battle of Gettysburg

http://www.collectorsnet.com/cwtimes/gettysbu.htm

For a description of the battle, casualty counts, a profile of General George
Meade, and other useful links

Military History Online—The Battle of Gettysburg

http://www.militaryhistoryonline.com/gettysburg/

For a detailed look at the three-day battle and information about modern-
day reenactments

Unofficial Visitor's Guide to Gettysburg

http://www.gettysburgguide.com/

For eyewitness accounts and essays about the battle and information about visiting the historic battlefield

Through the Mail

Gettysburg Convention and Visitors Bureau

35 Carlisle Street

Gettysburg, PA 17325

To get information about the Gettysburg National Military Park and the surrounding area

On the Road

Gettysburg National Military Park

97 Taneytown Road

Gettysburg, PA 17325

717/334-1124

To visit the site of the famous battle

INDEX

About the Author

Michael Burgan is a freelance writer for children and adults. A history graduate of the University of Connecticut, he has written more than thirty fiction and nonfiction children's books for various publishers. For adult audiences, he has written news articles, essays, and plays. Michael Burgan is a recipient of an Edpress Award and belongs to the Society of Children's Book Writers and Illustrators.